First World War
and Army of Occupation
War Diary
France, Belgium and Germany

27 DIVISION
Divisional Troops
1 Brigade Royal Field Artillery
23 November 1914 - 31 December 1915

WO95/2257/3

The Naval & Military Press Ltd
www.nmarchive.com
Published in association with The National Archives

Published by

The Naval & Military Press Ltd

Unit 10 Ridgewood Industrial Park,

Uckfield, East Sussex,

TN22 5QE England

Tel: +44 (0) 1825 749494

www.naval-military-press.com

www.nmarchive.com

This diary has been reprinted in facsimile from the original. Any imperfections are inevitably reproduced and the quality may fall short of modern type and cartographic standards.

© **Crown Copyright**
Images reproduced by permission of The National Archives, London, England, 2015.

Contents

Document type	Place/Title	Date From	Date To
Heading	WO95/2257/3		
Heading	27th Division Divl Artillery 1st Brigade R.F.A. Nov 1914-Dec 1915		
Heading	27th Division 1st Brigade R F A Vol I 23.11-31.12.14 Dec 1915		
War Diary	Magdalen Hill Camp Winchester	23/11/1914	31/12/1914
Heading	27th Division 1st Brigade R F A Vol II 1.1-28.2.15		
War Diary	Belgium	01/01/1915	28/02/1915
Heading	24th Division 1st Brigade R.F.A.Vol III 1-31.3.15		
War Diary	Belgium N W Of Vierstraat	01/03/1915	24/03/1915
Heading	27th Division 1st Brigade R F A Vol IV 1-30.4.15		
War Diary	Abeille	01/04/1915	01/04/1915
War Diary	East Of Ypres	05/04/1915	30/04/1915
Heading	27th Division 1st Brigade R F A Vol V 1-31.5.15		
War Diary	East Of Ypres	01/05/1915	31/05/1915
Heading	27th Division 1st Brigade R F A Vol VI 1-30.6.15		
War Diary	Armentieres	01/06/1915	30/06/1915
Heading	27th Division 1st Bde R F A Vol VII 1-31-7-15		
War Diary	Armentieres	01/07/1915	31/07/1915
Heading	27th Division 1st Bde R F A Vol VIII August 15		
War Diary	Armentieres	01/08/1915	31/08/1915
War Diary	Armentieres	28/08/1915	28/08/1915
Heading	27th Division 1st Bde R F A Vol IX Sep 1-15		
War Diary	Armentieres	01/09/1915	20/09/1915
War Diary	Cappy	01/10/1915	26/10/1915
War Diary	Cerisy	27/10/1915	29/10/1915
War Diary	Ferriere	31/10/1915	31/10/1915
Miscellaneous	Copied From Br. Gen. Stoke's Papers Recollections Of Ypres 1915		
Heading	27th Division 1st Bde R F A Nov Vol XI		
War Diary	Ferriere	01/11/1915	28/11/1915
War Diary	Pissy	29/11/1915	29/11/1915
Heading	27th 1st Bde R F A Dec Vol XII		
War Diary	Pissy	01/12/1915	09/12/1915
War Diary	Marseilles	31/12/1915	31/12/1915

W095 / 2257/3

27TH DIVISION
DIVL ARTILLERY

1ST BRIGADE R.F.A.

Nov ~~DEC~~ 1914 - DEC 1915

121/3872

27th Division.

1st Brigade R.F.A.

Vol I. 23.11 —— 31.12.14

Dec 1915

Army Form C. 2118.

WAR DIARY
or
INTELLIGENCE SUMMARY.
(Erase heading not required.)

Instructions regarding War Diaries and Intelligence Summaries are contained in F. S. Regs., Part II. and the Staff Manual respectively. Title pages will be prepared in manuscript.

Hour, Date, Place	Summary of Events and Information	Remarks and references to Appendices
MAGDALEN HILL CAMP WINCHESTER 23 Nov. 1914	The Brigade was formed on the 23rd November 1914 out of the 98th & 9 th R.F.A. Batteries. Transmit of HE. 97, 98, 132, 133rd Am.Col. and proceeded to mobilize on war establishments A.G. 1098-4C for a Brigade R.F.A. of H.B.Batteries each with 4.18pr Q.F.Guns. Major F.H.Stevenson, the senior officer Commanding	WD 2
Dec 3rd 1914	Lieut. Col. W. B. Emery joined & took over Command	WD 8
Dec. 20th 1914	The Brigade left Winchester as part of the 27th Div.Arty. to join the Expeditionary Force.	WD 8
Dec 21st 1914 12.30pm	Arrived HAVRE, camped at No 2 Camp.	WD 8
Dec 22nd 1914 8pm	Left HAVRE by train.	WD 8
Dec 23rd 1914 8pm	Arrived AIRE, marched to BOESGHEM, Billeted.	WD 8
Dec 31st 1914	Remained in same Billets	WD 8

121/4612

27th Division

1st Brigade, R.F.A.

Vol II. 1.1. – 28.2.15

Nil

Army Form C. 2118.

WAR DIARY
or
INTELLIGENCE SUMMARY.
(Erase heading not required.)

Instructions regarding War Diaries and Intelligence Summaries are contained in F.S. Regs., Part II. and the Staff Manual respectively. Title pages will be prepared in manuscript.

Hour, Date, Place	Summary of Events and Information	Remarks and references to Appendices
January 1915 BELGIUM		
1st Jan	Billetted at BOESEGHEN	WD2
5th —	Marched to PRADELLES	WD2
6th —	Marched to DICKEBUSCH. 48th Battery went into action replacing	WD2
7th —	a French Battery at 11 am. 13th Battery went into action replacing French Battery at 7 pm	WD2
21st —	The Brigade remained in action near VIERSTRAAT.	WD2
9th February	The 11th Battery joined the Brigade & remained in action	WD2
11th —	The Brigade supported the Infantry in the retaking of 4 trenches near ST ELOI from 4 pm until 6 am on 15th Feb.	WD2
28th —	Brigade remained in same position.	WD2

151/4919

27th Division

1st Brigade R.F.A.

1 – 31.3.15

WAR DIARY 1st Brigade R.F.A.
or
INTELLIGENCE SUMMARY.

Army Form C. 2118.

Instructions regarding War Diaries and Intelligence Summaries are contained in F. S. Regs., Part II. and the Staff Manual respectively. Title pages will be prepared in manuscript.

(Erase heading not required.)

Place	Hour, Date	Summary of Events and Information	Remarks and references to Appendices
BELGIUM N.W. of VIERSTRAAT	March 19 1915	Brigade was in action N.W. of VIERSTRAAT. The 39th Battery was attached for Tactical Purposes from the 19th R&O.R.F.A. Germans attacked at ST ELOI (3000 yards N.E. of Brigade)	WD & VOIR 7A
	1st 5:15 p.m. 14th	At 5:15 p.m. 3 light vevers and an explosion immediately followed. German guns opened & heavy rifle fire. Information was received at once from 9th Battery officer that Germans were attacking ST ELOI. The Brigade was ordered to open fire at once on the roads leading to ST ELOI.	WD2 VOIR 7A
	5:20 p.m.	Germans shelled Battery positions with High Explosive shell probably 5.9 for about half an hour. Smoke short.	
	15th hand 22nd 10 p.m.	Batteries continued to fire at intervals until 5 a.m. 11th, 132nd & 39th Batteries were withdrawn from action on relief by the 42nd Bde R.F.A. of 3rd Divn.	
	23rd 9:30 p.m.	The above Batteries & the Amn Column moved Billets to neighbourhood of POPERINGHE. ABEELE.	WD3 VOIR 7A
	24th 8/1915	The 96th & 133rd Batteries were relieved by 42nd Bde. The above Batteries rejoined the Brigade in Billets	W.T. Skinner Coronel R.F.A 1st Bde R.F.A

12/5318

29th Division

1st Brigade R.F.A.

Vol IV 1 – 30.4.15

Army Form C. 2118.

WAR DIARY
of 1st Brigade R.F.A
INTELLIGENCE SUMMARY.
(Erase heading not required.)

Instructions regarding War Diaries and Intelligence Summaries are contained in F.S. Regs., Part II. and the Staff Manual respectively. Title pages will be prepared in manuscript.

Hour, Date, Place	Summary of Events and Information	Remarks and references to Appendices
ABEILLE 1st April 1915	Brigade was resting	WD78
East of YPRES 5th April	Brigade relieved French Regiment of Artillery by sections (less 11th Battery) covering 81st Infantry Brigade	WD78
6th	Remaining Sections went into Action	WD78
8th	11th Battery came into action	WD78 / WD78
	the Brigade covered a zone from ZANDVOORDE to BECCELAERE. 148th Battalion being last by 19th B.212	WD78
9th	GERMAN Artillery very active	WD78
19th	GERMANS bombarded YPRES with very heavy Shell "13"	WD78
20th	GERMANS shelled details near using near channel which made eyes smart and had choking effect	WD78
22nd	Germans broke through French myth messages and advanced as far as the canal. 133rd Battery going to other end of canal and faced about. 145th also turned about	WD78
23rd	Brigade engaged enemy about St Julien	WD78
24th	Awoke to repel German attack on St Julien.	WD78
25th	Supported continued French and British attack on St JULIEN and wood to its West, from the S.E.	WD78
26th	Supported LAHORE Division in attack in same place from the South West	WD78

Army Form C. 2118.

WAR DIARY
or
INTELLIGENCE SUMMARY.
(Erase heading not required.)

Instructions regarding War Diaries and Intelligence Summaries are contained in F.S. Regs., Part II. and the Staff Manual respectively. Title pages will be prepared in manuscript.

Hour, Date, Place	Summary of Events and Information	Remarks and references to Appendices
April 27th	Germans shelled our positions from East, North & WEST	
28th	Our Artillery bombarded wood N. of ST. JULIEN.	
29th	Germans replied with heavy guns from about position	
30th	98th and 133rd position as noted heavily shelled from West & East. Nothing particular happened, shelling continued.	With during all the above informed the Wagon lines ammunitions through. KEMP's men down MEDS shelled and many ... caused 1st Army fld. A.78 Coney Lt. Roy. Arts.

29th Division.

1st Brigade R.F.A.

Vol I 1 — 31.5.16

Army Form C. 2118.

WAR DIARY
of 1st Brigade R.F.A.
INTELLIGENCE SUMMARY. MAY 1915.
(Erase heading not required.)

Instructions regarding War Diaries and Intelligence Summaries are contained in F.S. Regs., Part II. and the Staff Manual respectively. Title pages will be prepared in manuscript.

Hour, Date, Place	Summary of Events and Information	Remarks and references to Appendices
East of YPRES 1st May 1915	Brigade in position near BELLEWARDE Lake 11th, 46th and 132nd covering the South East 133 and 116 (attached) covering ground between	
9 p.m.	GRAVENSTAFEL and ST JULIEN. Germans shelled all Batteries at 13.9.14.a north 6" H.E. 1 Section par Battery was withdrawn and placed in New Position nearer YPRES.	WTS 2
2nd May	Germans shelled positions at intervals	
9 p.m.	Withdrew remaining sections formed those in position nearer YPRES (except 11th Battery which maintained one Section in original position. The Brigade now covered a zone from a point about 500 yards South of MENIN ROAD, to the Railway to ZONNEBEKE. The 19th Bde covered the ground to the Right. The 28th Divisional Artillery covered the ground to the Left. The retirement was completed without incident. Brigade Hd Qrs were established on the Railway about ½ mile N.W. of MENIN ROAD.	WTS 2

Army Form C. 2118.

WAR DIARY
or
INTELLIGENCE SUMMARY.
(Erase heading not required.)

Instructions regarding War Diaries and Intelligence Summaries are contained in F.S. Regs., Part II. and the Staff Manual respectively. Title pages will be prepared in manuscript.

Hour, Date, Place	Summary of Events and Information	Remarks and references to Appendices
2nd May 1915	Germans opened very heavy fire from guns of all calibres in every direction and maintained it all day. German Infantry gradually approached, and owing to lack of precautions in not destroying houses, woods and other strong posts close to our Infantry line, before retiring, the Batteries were constantly called upon to fire at such places when the enemy naturally occupied them.	WB2
3rd May 1915	Germans shelled positions very heavily. Found the keeping up Telephonic communications hopeless as wires were cut continually.	1 killed & wounded WB2
4th May 1915	ditto	1 wounded WB2
5th May 1915	Fired at intervals all day in reply to German shelling of our Infantry Trenches.	1 wounded
6th May 1915	Fired all day at intervals to protect Infantry from German shelling.	WB2 1 killed 4 wounded
7th May	party quiet.	WB2 1 wounded
8th May	132 was placed hors de combat by two salvoes from German 5.9 gun and withdrawn at night.	WB2 1 killed 4 wounded

WAR DIARY
or
INTELLIGENCE SUMMARY.

1st Brigade R.H.A.
May 1915

Army Form C. 2118.

Hour, Date, Place	Summary of Events and Information	Remarks and references to Appendices
9th May 1915	Fairly quiet.	
10th May 1915	Germans shelled 3rd K.R.Rs out of their trenches in HOOGE CHATEAU WOOD and they fell back to Eastern Edge. The whole line of Infantry Trenches from HOOGE to VERLORENHOEK was heavily shelled. Major Stevenson D.S.O. 98th Battery was severely wounded and the 98th Battery so badly shelled that it was withdrawn at night and the 98th Battery brought into action between the Railway and the MENIN ROAD.	W732 4 killed 15 wounded W732 3 wounded 1 killed
11th May	Germans attacked along MENIN ROAD and 9 annual come ground. 4th Durham Howitzer Battery brought one section into action close to Railway on North Side.	W732 killed 9 wounded
12th May	Fairly quiet.	W712
13th May	Germans shelled Cavalry out of their trenches from BELLEGATDE to VERLORENHOEK. Batteries fired all day. 99th and Lof. H. Batteries did great execution from their advanced positions. Moved H.Q. to East side of Canal on DICKEBUSCH Road	W732 2 wounded

Army Form C. 2118.

WAR DIARY
or ~~Intelligence Summary~~ of [ ] Brigade R.F.A.

May 1915

(Erase heading not required.)

Instructions regarding War Diaries and Intelligence Summaries are contained in F.S. Regs., Part II. and the Staff Manual respectively. Title pages will be prepared in manuscript.

Hour, Date, Place	Summary of Events and Information	Remarks and references to Appendices
East of YPRES 14th May 1915	Fairly quiet. Batteries shelled farms & posts in rear of German lines	1 wounded
15th	Very quiet	WTB? 1st Bde Zone extended from 500 yards S of MENIN ROAD to North edge of BELLEWARDE Lake
16th	Quiet Day. N.B. During the above period from the 2nd May the command of the artillery in action of 27th Ind Arty East of YPRES was handed over to Lt Colonel W.B. Emery Comdg 1st Brigade R.F.A under directions of C.R.A. On this day the C.R.A 27th Divl Arty resumed command	WTB?
17th	Moved H.Q. to Eastern Ramparts of YPRES.	1 missing 19th 1 wounded 22nd 2 wounded
18th – 23rd	Fairly quiet.	
24th	Germans attacked at 2.45am with gas and Heavy Artillery all along front from MENIN ROAD to RAILWAY and broke through on the South side of the RAILWAY. North of BELLEWARDE Lake in 28 Divl Arty Zone. Counterattacks failed owing to lack of organization and co-operation between Cavalry Bn'd Ch'n Inf'y notes	WTB? Brigade fired 6000 rounds. 2 wounded 1 killed

Army Form C. 2118.

WAR DIARY
or
INTELLIGENCE SUMMARY.

(Erase heading not required.)

18/Brigade RFA May 1915

Hour, Date, Place	Summary of Events and Information	Remarks and references to Appendices
East of YPRES 25th May 1915	Brigade formed certain round HOOGE at request of G.O.C. 3rd Cavalry Brigade	WXL 2 inf.Mch 4 wounded
26th - 28th	Fairly quiet.	WXL
29th	1 Section Battery was relieved by sections of 20th Brigade except 135th Battery which moved complete (3 guns) and marched to ARMENTIÈRES at 10 a.m. to ARMENTIÈRES	
30th	Remainder relieved and marched on the night went into action where the sections relieved on the night went into action East of the Town.	WXL
31st	Remainder of Brigade went in to action (less 11th Battery) H.Q. on LILLE ROAD.	WX2

W.B.Emery
Lt Col R.A.
Comdg. 18 Bde RFA

27th Division

12/6033

1st Brigade R.F.A.

Vol VI 1—30.6.15.

Army Form C. 2118.

WAR DIARY
or 1st BRIGADE
INTELLIGENCE SUMMARY. R.F.A. June 1915

(Erase heading not required.)

Instructions regarding War Diaries and Intelligence Summaries are contained in F.S. Regs., Part II and the Staff Manual respectively. Title pages will be prepared in manuscript.

Hour, Date, Place	Summary of Events and Information	Remarks and references to Appendices
ARMENTIÈRES June 1st – 30th	The Brigade remained in action during unusually at localities or anything special etc. The Germans doing the same. The Brigade zone extended from RUE DU BOIS to the Railway to PERENCHIES. Nothing of importance occurred The opportunity was taken to have all the guns overhauled. Two men were slightly wounded by shell splinters. W.H. Onslow Lt. Col. R.A. Comdg 1st Bde R.F.A.	175²

27th Division

121/6390

1st Bde. R.F.A.

Vol VII

1-31-4-15

Army Form C. 2118.

WAR DIARY 1ST BRIGADE
or
INTELLIGENCE SUMMARY. R.F.A.

(Erase heading not required.)

July 1915

Hour, Date, Place	Summary of Events and Information	Remarks and references to Appendices
ARMENTIÈRES 1st to 18th July	The Brigade remained in action as before. Nothing of importance occurred.	6752
19th July to 31st July	Brigade formed part of "B" group with the 99th, 364th, & 6/5th (How) Batteries covering 81st Infantry Brigade in trenches from RUE DUBOIS to WEZ MACQUART. Nothing of importance occurred.	6752
31st July 6.30 pm	At 6.30 pm "B" group carried out a small bombardment of German trenches about RUE DUBOIS in cooperation with 2nd Gloucesters. No casualties occurred. During the month 1 man 98th Battery was wounded by a bullet when exercising a horse.	6752

W.T. Furey
Lt Col R.F.A
Comg 1st Bde R F A

27th Division

1st Bde R.F.A.
Vol VIII
August 15

2039/121

WAR DIARY 1st Brigade R.F.A.
or
INTELLIGENCE SUMMARY. August 1915

Army Form C. 2118.

Hour, Date, Place	Summary of Events and Information	Remarks and references to Appendices
ARMENTIÈRES August 1st 5.20 pm	The batteries of "B" group & 27th Divisional Artillery with the cooperation of three batteries "A" group and the 2nd Howitzer Regiment carried out a combined demonstration against the German position at RUE-DU-BOIS. The four batteries of the First Brigade formed part of "B" Group". The object of the operations was (1) To cut wire and damage enemy's parapets. (2) To induce the Germans to man their trenches in order to hit them. (3) To gain instruction in methods of attack and information about the enemy. The 11th and 98th batteries were detailed for wire cutting, but owing to his immense amount of cover carried by his trenches shooting resulted by the howitzer amount of ammunition allowed and to the limited amount of ammunition allowed. After the weeks of his operations this report were disappointing. The wire cutting was over, the 1st Brigade batteries joined in a general bombardment of the enemy's trenches for ten minutes, the fire of his batteries appeared to be accurate and his fuzes appeared to be drawn accurately.	1st Brigade R.F.A. plot 155 ends 14 pages
6.30/-	After a short pause in order to enable our infantry, who had been with drawn, to re-occupy the fire trenches, fire was again opened on the enemy's trenches—communications

WAR DIARY or INTELLIGENCE SUMMARY.

(Erase heading not required.)

Army Form C. 2118.

1st Brigade R.F.A.

August 1915

Hour, Date, Place	Summary of Events and Information	Remarks and references to Appendices
ARMENTIERES August 1st	and the infantry opened rapid fire, in order to make the enemy believe that an assault was about to be delivered by us. Operations began at 5.20 pm and concluded at about 6.30 pm.	
10 pm	At 10 pm all batteries engaged with the exception of 98 B fired 2 salvos on to the enemy's trenches. The infantry reported that they were of opinion that the effect was satisfactory as the enemy were at the time repairing the damage done by the bombardment of the afternoon. For the operations the 98 B battery ran a section forward to a range of about 2000 yards or even to 1500 entering	WD2
Aug 2nd – 31st	The Brigade remained in action covering the left Brigade of Infantry of the 27th Division. Nothing of importance occurred. All interior communications btwn gun portions and prepared alternative ones.	WD2
28 Aug	On the 28th August Lieut Gen. O. In Cmmd 132 Battery was killed by enemy shell fire in the RUE DUFAUBOURG DE LILLE ARMENTIERES.	WD2

(Sgd) [signature]
Comdg 1st Bde RFA

27th Division

1st Bde R.F.A.
Bolix
Sept 15

WAR DIARY
INTELLIGENCE SUMMARY

1st Brigade R.F.A.

Army Form C. 2118.

September 1915

(Erase heading not required.)

Instructions regarding War Diaries and Intelligence Summaries are contained in F.S. Regs., Part II. and the Staff Manual respectively. Title pages will be prepared in manuscript.

Hour, Date, Place	Summary of Events and Information	Remarks and references to Appendices
1st Sept. ARMENTIÈRES	Brigade Transport work on.	
12th Sept.	132nd Battery fired 120 rounds H.E at German Salient in RUE DU BOIS from a position N.W of CHAPELLE d'ARMENTIÈRES for Experimental purposes	
13th Sept.	132nd Battery fired 100 rounds H.E. } for experimental 133rd Battery fired 230 rounds H.E. } purposes	
14th Sept.	The Batteries were withdrawn out of action to the wagon lines West of ARMENTIÈRES being relieved by 104th Brigade R.F.A.	
15th Sept.	Brigade marched to Billets at MOOLENAECKER.	
16 Sept.	Rest and Route marching	
17 Sept.	"	
18 Sept.	Route marching	
19 Sept.	Entrained at STEEN BECQUE for AMIENS	W.R. knows V. 106 V.A
20 Sept.	11th 95th & 132nd Batteries brought one section each into action E. of CAPPY relieving the French. Remainder of Brigade brought in to action.	Army, Letter 01A.

Army Form C. 2118.

WAR DIARY
or
INTELLIGENCE SUMMARY.
(Erase heading not required.)

October 1915   1st Brigade R.F.A.

2199/166

Hour. Date. Place	Summary of Events and Information	Remarks and references to Appendices
25th	Very quiet. The Brigade remained in action covering the 82nd Infantry Brigade in the Trenches.	
25th	One section per Battery of 11th 98th & 132nd Batteries were relieved by Batteries of the 22nd Regt of the French 6th Army and retired to wagon lines	A good deal of H.E.
6th	Remaining Sections and 133 Battery withdrawn but the Brigade moved to CERISY (5 miles) Resting at CERISY	
7th		
1st Nov	Brigade marched to BOVES. (15 miles)	
2nd	Brigade marched to neighbourhood of FERRIÈRE	
3rd Nov	Brigade remained in billets	Very wet.

WS Lucey
Lt Col Comdg 1st Bde RFA

2 Nov 1915

Copied from Br.- GEN. STOKE'S PAPERS.

RECOLLECTIONS OF YPRES 1915.

1st Brigade R.F.A. - Lt.-Colonel W.B. Emery, R.F.A.

Commanding.

---

1. The Brigade consisted of

    H.Q., 98th, 132nd and 133rd Batteries,
    Brigade Ammunition Column.

Went into action East of YPRES on Easter Monday, 5th April 1915. The 11th Battery joined the Brigade on the 8th April.

POSITIONS. Brigade H.Q. in Farm ¼ mile N.E. of BELLEWAARDE Farm.

    98th and 133rd Batteries in the east edges of a small wood 300 yards North of Brigade H.Q.

    132nd Battery in echelon in a wood N. of BELLEWAARDE Pond.

    The 11th Battery in Railway Wood.

    The last-named battery was the only one which had any protection. Major Robertson immediately began to dig in his guns and detachments in the raised mound on which the wood stands, and made his position fairly proof against small shell.

    The Brigade Zone originally covered the line HERENTHAGE - POLYGON WOOD. The wagon lines were about 1 mile west of POTIJZE south of the main road. Some German guns annoyed our Infantry near HERENTHAGE by enfilade fire which was extremely accurate and dangerous.

    Two guns of 98th Battery were placed near WESTHOEK which enfiladed the opposing German Trenches so effectively that the German guns shut up.

    Our Infantry lines of trenches remained in the same positions HERENTHAGE - POLYGON WOOD until ordered to retire to the G.H.Q. line on May 2nd/3rd.

    On Sunday 18th April the Germans began to bombard the town of YPRES with very heavy shell.

On 20th April Germans used Tear Shell on our positions for the first time.

On the 22nd April the Germans attacked the French on our left and rear, and broke through to the Canal. At night the limbers were kept near the guns in case of accidents. The 148th Howitzer Battery had meanwhile been attached to the Brigade and was in action West of BELLEWAARDE Pond.

On the 23rd April the 133rd and 148th Batteries were turned round to fire North.

On the 24th the Germans attacked ST. JULIEN.

During the next few days there was heavy fighting about ST. JULIEN and a wood West of St. Julien.

My chief recollection of this time is the fact that the 148th Howitzer Battery had to shoot WEST, NORTH & EAST.

The 133rd faced WEST in the Western edge of their small wood; whilst the 98th Battery had a section shooting NORTH and another N.E. from the same wood.

The 132nd Battery alone continued to support our 27th Division Infantry.

The Wood, about 200 yards long by 100 yards broad in which the 133rd and 98th were, was shelled continuously, luckily by shrapnel which burst on the tree tops or were buried. The Batteries suffered very few casualties although not entrenched. The ground did not admit digging.

The Tear Shell were a nuisance.

The hollow in which the 148th was became full of fumes. Also the dug outs in RAILWAY WOOD became untenable.

Brigade H.Q. although in full view of the enemy and constantly shelled, from WEST, NORTH & EAST, was not actually hit.

Telephone Lines were perpetually being cut.

German aeroplanes were very in evidence, flying low and observing at leisure.

I saw one brought down by our Infantry Fire.

During this time one gun of 132nd in a wood absolutely enfilading the MENIN ROAD was most useful in preventing the Germans using that road.

On Monday 26th April the Lahore Division attempted to retake a wood west of ST. JULIEN but made no progress.

Fighting continued about the wood on the 27th and 28th during which time the Germans maintained a heavy fire from a large number of guns.

On the 29th April, the wagon lines were sent back to the West of YPRES near VLAMERTINGHE. They had suffered very heavy casualties.

On Friday 30th April I went to Division H.Q. and was instructed to withdraw to positions nearer YPRES facing north.

My Brigade H.Q. had meanwhile been moved to some dugouts in a Railway Cutting owing to communications with the Farm becoming impossible.

On 1st May one section per Battery was withdrawn to positions nearer Ypres; 98th in a hedge in the open just north of the Railway line about 1 mile east of Railway Crossing on MENIN ROAD, 132nd and 133rd North of MENIN Road opposite l'Ecole de Bienfaisance. The 11th Battery near the LILLE GATE E. of the Ramparts. On the night of the 1st/2nd the Germans kept up very heavy shell fire on all roads. Orders had been issued to carry out the retirement on this night, but were cancelled. This was a curious coincidence. A general retirement under such a fire would have entailed heavy losses.

On the night of the 2nd/3rd May the general retirement to the line roughly BELLEWAARDE Pond - VERLORENHOEK was carried out in absolute peace. The remaining sections were retired to new positions.

Soon after dawn on the 3rd May the Germans advanced

cautiously under heavy covering fire of artillery, until they came in contact with our new line. Brigade H.Q. remained in dugouts on the railway.

The New Line had the serious disadvantage from an artillery point of view, that the high ground WESTHOEK ridge was given up. Observation of fire became difficult. We had no aeroplanes co-operating.

The Germans were very successful in setting fire to farms with incendiary shell. Their shooting was extraordinarily accurate. Two or three shell sufficed to put a farm into a blaze. For From our H.Q. we watched many farms set on fire.

On May 4th German shelling was very heavy and made our communications hopeless by telephone. Runners were the only possible method.

On 5th May Germans shelled our Infantry trenches all day. We had no means of stopping them as they were all under cover and observation was impossible.

Our Brigade fire was directed onto such enemy infantry as were visible.

Our Batteries were not spotted by the Germans until the 8th May when the area about 132nd and 133rd was very heavily shelled. Most of 133 guns were put out of action. 132 escaped punishment until a premature gave away their exact position, when they were quickly put out of action by extremely accurate fire from 5.9" howitzers, losing many of the detachments.

133 withdrew at dusk to a new position close to the Ramparts. 132 was withdrawn also.

On 10th May Germans shelled 3rd K.R.R's out of their trenches in HOOGE CHATEAU WOODS. They fell back to the rear of the Woods. 98th Battery was badly shelled. This battery did good work all day and greatly impeded the German advance down the Railway. Firing over the sights at about

1000 yards.

Major Stevenson was wounded. The Battery suffered many casualties and was withdrawn to rest, at dusk, being replaced temporarily by the 99th Battery.

I would here mention that the Brigade H.Q. was in front of the battery positions, being in a cutting, on the railway. On the 8th May Telephone lines were cut continually and the only means of conveying order to batteries was by sending officers. Eventually all other officers being away I had to go myself to the 132nd and 133rd Batteries to direct them onto the enemy's infantry who were making considerable progress, and I was thus an eyewitness of the sudden overwhelming of the 132nd Battery by a few well-directed salvoes of 5.9's.

On May 11th, owing to the impossibility of keeping telephonic communication up, H.Q. was moved to the East side of the Canal at KRUISSTRAAT. The railway dugouts being kept as an O.P. for use by day. On this day the 4th Durham Light Howitzer Battery of 5-in. Hows. came into action. Owing to their short range it was essential to put them forward and the only places that offered any cover was the same hedge in which the 98th Battery had suffered so badly; but they were able to fire from a point nearer the railway. As a matter of fact the Germans continued to shell the old 98th position but never found the 4th Durhams who did very good work.

On May 13th the 2nd Cavalry Division was fiercely attacked and fairly shelled out of their trenches from VERLORENHOEK to BELLEGARDE. The cavalry suffered severely but maintained their ground. General de Lisle sent me a very complimentary letter thanking the gunners for the support given.

I would mention that a section of 4.7-in guns was in action under my command at this time, but owing to their condition and bad ammunition I had to stop them from firing anywhere near our own line.

May 14th, 15th, 16th to 23rd were fairly quiet.

On 15th May I shewed Major Chapman of the 5th. Durham How. Battery round the position. Also Colonel Stockley Commanding Durham Brigade.

May 17th. Finding Brigade H.Q. too far from the Batteries, it was moved into the Ramparts close to the Sally Port e. of Menin Gate, where it remained until we left Ypres.

Monday 24th May. The Germans attacked at 2.30 a.m. with gas and shell all along the line; and broke in between Hooge and the Railway.

They did not penetrate beyond the woods, and I think there is no doubt that their advance was held up mainly by the fire of the 1st Brigade R.F.A. Hooge Chateau was held throughout by a Cavalry detachment, but I have been informed by eye-witnesses that between that point and Bellwarde the Artillery fire practically prevented the enemy's advance far south of the Pond.

The Gas was very trying as we had only indifferent respirators.

My own Staff were nearly all more or less overcome. Personally I kept a wet silk handkerchief over my face as much as possible, smoked most of the day and suffered no ill effects. The batteries were firing hard all day. Lucklily they were well concealed and only a few guns were put out of action.

I remember one gun of 133rd Battery was hit by a 5.9 shell and only the gun itself was left intact, upside down on a very twisted trail.

6a.

As a matter of interest I recount the following episode.

About 3.30 p.m. I received a message by telephone ordering me to meet Br.-General X at the Lille Gate at 4 o'clock.

I could not gain any more information. I was at the Lille Gate at 4 o'clock and whilst waiting for the General wandered about and found infantry lying down in column along the Canal Bank. I could get no information from them as all the officers were away at a pow-wow. I tried to get through to the Div. H.Q. from a telephone centre just across the bridge with a view to finding out what was going on, but could not.

Eventually Br.-General X arrived about 6.30 p.m. and informed me that he had been ordered to make a counter attack on the Line HOOGE - BELLEWAARDE, in conjunction with another brigade, starting at 7 p.m. (I think) to turn the Germans out. He had been ordered to have his H.Q. at the Lille Gate. *I was acting C.R.A. north of Ypres 24th*

Division at the time, and had lines out connecting me to the F.O.Os. and Infantry. There was no communication from the Lille Gate. My lines were mostly cut but still were better than nothing. It was a matter of difficulty to arrange connection with and support for a counter-attack at half hour's notice after a very hard day's fighting.

A line was laid by my telephonists to the Infantry Brigade H.Q. at Lille Gate. I managed to find an Officer to act as liaison with the Infantry attacking line. N.B. The officer was a last joined Subaltern from the Shop and had been in France about a week. The guns had been shooting at the point of attack all day, so presumably had the range fairly accurately. As a matter of fact, the two Infantry Brigades failed to make liaiaon, owing I believe to the severe losses sustained en route to the points of assembly. One Brigade went up the Railway which was an absolute death trap. Anyway I was able to maintain conversation with my F.O.O. throughout the night, and, happening to know the country well, to direct him by telephone where to go and what to do, and from his reports to judge the rate of fire required from time to time. He was able to tell me what was going on.

Unfortunately the counter-attack failed, owing I think to the darkness of the night which rendered any exercise of command impossible. I have always been convinced that if more time had been allowed for preparation of co-operation between the two Infantry Brigades and the guns, a counter-attack would have been successful.

In the 27th Division the liaison between guns and infantry was close, and xxx we always knew what the Infantry were doing and what they wanted us to do.

During this second battle of Ypres, on the other hand, as far as my experience went, we suffered from being left in complete ignorance of what Infantry were coming into our area, and what they were trying to do.

On several occasions, at dawn, I found a new Brigade or Division had arrived in the Salient which my Brigade was more or less covering, without any information having been vouchsafed as to their name, position of H.Q. or intentions.   By the time I had managed to discover what they were doing it was generally too late to help them in any way.

Unfortunately they soon melted away under the German gun fire to which we could make no reply.

The supply of ammunition was ordinarily replenished by night.   The only available route was through the town of Ypres and during the active bombardment, the Ammunition Column and Battery Wagons suffered many casualties.

Much credit was due to the personnel for their unfailing courage and energy.   On some occasions it was necessary to replenish ammunition by day.

I cannot remember what the Brigade's casualties amounted to.   Three Majors had to be replaced of whom 1 was wounded, 2 went sick.   About 250 horses were killed.

The lack of heavy guns to deal with the German guns was a serious drawback.   Our aeroplanes were conspicuous by their absence.

The Germans used large numbers of Balloons for observation which greatly annoyed us as we could not reach them.

The Brigade left Ypres on the night of the 30th-31st May for Armentieres and took over from the 24th Brigade on the night of the 31st May - 1st June.

(Sd)   W.B.EMERY,
Br.-General.

27th Harrow

1st Bde. R.F.A.

764 / X / 764

121 / 7694

WAR DIARY
or
INTELLIGENCE SUMMARY.
(Erase heading not required.)

Army Form C. 2118.

NOVEMBER 1915

1st Brigade R.F.A.

Hour, Date, Place	Summary of Events and Information	Remarks and references to Appendices
FERRIÈRE 1st to 28th Nov.	Brigade remained in Billets about FERRIÈRE On 6th Nov. The Brigade was reorganised on Special Establishments for SALONIKA FORCE "3".	Capt. C.T. Bates 11th Battery left the Brigade on 4.11.15. Capt. & Adjt. W.E. Delves-Broughton and Capt. J.O. Naismith 11th Battery, G.T.A. left the Brigade on 6.11.15.
29th Nov PISSY	Brigade moved into new Billets about PISSY W.T. Furey Lt. Col. R.F.A. Comdg. 1st Bde R.F.A.	Capt. E.W.G. Wilson joined on 11.11.15 and was posted to 11th Battery R.F.A. Lieut. W. Scott-Watson joined the S.A.A. Column on 7.11.15. 2/Lt. Draper W.P. joined S.A.A. Col on 15.11.15

1st Bde. R.F.A.

WAR DIARY DECEMBER 1915 Army Form C. 2118.
or
INTELLIGENCE SUMMARY. 1st Brigade R.F.A.

(Erase heading not required.)

Instructions regarding War Diaries and Intelligence Summaries are contained in F. S. Regs., Part II and the Staff Manual respectively. Title pages will be prepared in manuscript.

Hour, Date, Place	Summary of Events and Information	Remarks and references to Appendices
1st December — 7th PISSY	The Brigade remained in Billets	21st Nov. Major A.G. LEECH Comdg 98th Battery R.F.A. assumed Command of the Brigade Temporarily during the time that Lt Colonel W.B. Browne was acting C.R.A. 27th Division, up to 31.12.15
7th Dec.	The Brigade entrained at LONGEAU for MARSEILLES	
9th Dec. MARSEILLES	The Brigade arrived at MARSEILLES and went on to Camp at BORELY Camp where it remained during the rest of the month awaiting embarkation	
31st Dec		

A.G. Leech R.F.A.
Commanding 1st Brigade R.F.A.